A Hostile Environment

A Hostile Environment

Nigel Kent & Sarah Thomson

A Poetry Conversation

First published 2019 by The Hedgehog Poetry Press,

5 Coppack House, Churchill Avenue, Clevedon. BS21 6QW

www.hedgehogpress.co.uk

Copyright © Nigel Kent & Sarah Thomson 2019. The right of Nigel Kent & Sarah Thomson to be identified as the authors of this work has been asserted in accordance with the Copyright, Designs and Patents Act 1988. All rights reserved. No part of this publication may be reproduced, stored in or introduced into a retrieval system, or transmitted in any form, or by any means (electronic, mechanical, photocopying, recording or otherwise) without prior written permissions of the publisher. Any person who does any unauthorised act in relation to this publication may be liable for criminal prosecution and civil claims for damages. All the characters in this publication are fictitious and any resemblance to real persons, living or dead, is purely coincidental.

ISBN: 978-1-9164806-5-0

First published 2019 by The Hedgehog Poetry Press,

5 Coppack House, Churchill Avenue, Clevedon. BS21 6QW

www.hedgehogpress.co.uk

Copyright © Nigel Kent & Sarah Thomson 2019. The right of Nigel Kent & Sarah Thomson to be identified as the authors of this work has been asserted in accordance with the Copyright, Designs and Patents Act 1988. All rights reserved. No part of this publication may be reproduced, stored in or introduced into a retrieval system, or transmitted in any form, or by any means (electronic, mechanical, photocopying, recording or otherwise) without prior written permissions of the publisher. Any person who does any unauthorised act in relation to this publication may be liable for criminal prosecution and civil claims for damages. All the characters in this publication are fictitious and any resemblance to real persons, living or dead, is purely coincidental.

ISBN: 978-1-9164806-5-0

A Hostile Environment

Nigel Kent & Sarah Thomson

A Poetry Conversation

Contents

1. A Hostile Environment	8
2. Splinters (A Golden Shovel)	9
3. Instruction for removal	10
4. Too late for the vaquitas	11
5. Crossed	12
6. The Migrants	14

In the summer of 2018 the story broke of the mistreatment of members of the Windrush generation. As a consequence of the government's attempts to reduce immigration, it transpired that British subjects had been wrongly deported and detained, lost their jobs and homes, and were denied benefits and medical treatment. This story precipitated a poetry conversation.

A Hostile Environment

She stands before his desk
but he does not see her.

His hand dismisses testimony
taken from her bag for life,

He jams questions
between her clenched teeth:

cold, rigid and iron heavy,
crushing answers.

He cuffs her wrists
with new rules, rivet tight.

Each stroke of his pen
inflicts blue indelible welts.

She takes away his form
filled with rows of crosses.

She watches them burn through the night.
At dawn her door splinters.

Splinters (A Golden Shovel)

We came on the Windrush, called it our 'ship of hope'. At

                The time we thought we would be welcome. It was to be our new
                Dawn

It rained a lot. Some people wished us gone. Even so, I got my passport. Our little girl was born. Her

  Arrival changed everything. Made our hearts sing. I thought the nightmares gone. Until her call. Administrative removal. Our precious daughter. Nothing makes
                        sense anymore. The wolf is through the Door.

We came on the Windrush. Our 'ship of hope'. Shattered. Broken into tiny pieces. Everything in Splinters.

Instruction for removal

When the foxgloves appeared in the rectory garden,
transported across its borders by rush of wind and water,
the vicar welcomed them, and harvested their seeds,
sowing them in every shady corner,
where they thrived in carnivals of colour.
Till the dark mutterings of neighbours started:
finger-pointing warnings of danger to his daughter;
finger-wagging reminders of his duty to contain
their advance within his boundary walls.
The girl watched her father's gloved hands fell
the splendid spires and tear the roots from the soil,
tossing them to rot on the compost heap,
to feed the gratitude that would soon blossom in the parish.

Today, grown-up, the daughter sits in her office
piles of deportation orders before her,
the sulphurous stench of mulch stinging her nostrils.

Instruction for removal

When the foxgloves appeared in the rectory garden,
transported across its borders by rush of wind and water,
the vicar welcomed them, and harvested their seeds,
sowing them in every shady corner,
where they thrived in carnivals of colour.
Till the dark mutterings of neighbours started:
finger-pointing warnings of danger to his daughter;
finger-wagging reminders of his duty to contain
their advance within his boundary walls.
The girl watched her father's gloved hands fell
the splendid spires and tear the roots from the soil,
tossing them to rot on the compost heap,
to feed the gratitude that would soon blossom in the parish.

Today, grown-up, the daughter sits in her office
piles of deportation orders before her,
the sulphurous stench of mulch stinging her nostrils.

Splinters (A Golden Shovel)

We came on the Windrush, called it our 'ship of hope'. At

>The time we thought we would be welcome. It was to be our new
>Dawn

It rained a lot. Some people wished us gone. Even so, I got my passport. Our little girl was born. Her

>Arrival changed everything. Made our hearts sing. I thought the nightmares gone. Until her call. Administrative removal. Our precious daughter. Nothing makes sense anymore. The wolf is through the Door.

We came on the Windrush. Our 'ship of hope'. Shattered. Broken into tiny pieces. Everything in Splinters.

Too late for the vaquitas

Sign your name to save the planet, put your cross in the right places
Find an acorn grow a tree, they're felling forests while you sleep
Send your money to good causes, seed bomb long abandoned spaces
Sign your name to save the planet, put your cross in the right places
It's too late for the vaquitas, late at night you'll see their faces
Miles and miles of plastic floating on the ocean watch and weep
Sign your name to save the planet, put your cross in the right places
Find an acorn grow a tree, they're felling forests while you sleep

Crossed

This is the cross that cast the vote.

This is the cross that cast the vote
that put the party in power.

This is the cross that cast the vote
that put the party in power
to cut immigration.

This is the cross that cast the vote
that put the party in power
to pass the laws
to cut immigration.

This is the cross that cast the vote
that put the party in power
to pass the laws
that lost him his job
to cut immigration.

This is the cross that cast the vote
that put the party in power
to pass the laws
that lost him his job
that left him in debt
to cut immigration.

This is the cross that cast the vote
that put the party in power
to pass the laws
that lost him his job
that left him in debt
that cost him his home
to cut immigration.

This is the cross that cast the vote
that put the party in power
to pass the laws
that lost him his job
that left him in debt
that cost him his home
that wrecked his health
to cut immigration.

This is the cross that cast the vote
that put the party in power
to pass the laws
that lost him his job
that left him in debt
that cost him his home
that wrecked his health
that denied him drugs
to cut immigration.

This is the cross that cast the vote
that put the party in power
to pass the laws
that lost him his job
that left him in debt
that cost him his home
that wrecked his health
that denied him drugs
that took his life
to cut immigration.

This is the vote that crossed the line
to cut immigration and save the nation!

The Migrants

They arrived early morning in a container.
I gave them shelter. There were five of them.
They were no trouble, just ate and slept,
Didn't want to talk. They were dark
And very small, not much like me at all,
But still with that same need to stay alive.

It was worrying at the time. Looking
Back I can see it was in fact a miracle.
They began to grow so fast they had to
Shed their skin. Two thrived, one hid,
Two stayed thin. They spun silk for seven
Days, ensnared themselves then hung.

It was a shock. Rain fell, the temperature
Dropped. I wrapped a blanket round
Their box. They made no sound. For
Seven days the earth turned round.
On the eighth a bug appeared, unfurled
Amber wings, bled bright drops of red.

Next day another three. I brought them
Fruit and flowers as they convalesced.
They let me know when they were good
To go. Outside two flapped to the ground
Two gave thanks, cried freedom, skywards
Soared until too high for the eye to see.

Shy number five revealed herself when
All the rest had gone. I'll keep her one day
More. She may drop or she may soar.
They weren't born equal. All I can do is
Offer hospitality before the long flight south,
Fight to keep the environment right.

Sarah Thomson

Sarah grew up by the sea in Weymouth, Dorset and now lives in Bristol. She developed a love for writing from an early age and studied English at the University of Exeter. After a varied career in publishing, accountancy and Human Resources, Sarah is now a full-time writer of poetry, novels and lyrics. In 2017 she was shortlisted for the Bridport Prize and a winner of the Persimmon International Poets Competition. Her poem 'Mercy' was highly commended by The Hedgehog Poetry Press and published in *The Road to Clevedon Pier* in 2018.

Nigel Kent

Nigel is a reader and writer of poetry who lives in Worcestershire. He has been shortlisted for a number of poetry prizes but has not yet won one! His poetry has been published by Hedgehog Poetry Press, Dempsey and Windle, Paper Swan Press, Emma's Attic Publishing, the Poetry Society of the Open University, Fly on the Wall Poetry Press and Eye Flash Poetry.

He generally writes free verse and is an admirer of the work of Ted Kooser, Steve Kowit, Stephen Dobyns, Gary Soto, Kim Addonizio, Maggie Sawkins, Luke Wright, Tony Walsh Michael Meyerhofer and , of course, Sarah Thomson! Currently he is working on a collection of poetry written in response to his favourite paintings.

Sarah Thomson

Sarah grew up by the sea in Weymouth, Dorset and now lives in Bristol. She developed a love for writing from an early age and studied English at the University of Exeter. After a varied career in publishing, accountancy and Human Resources, Sarah is now a full-time writer of poetry, novels and lyrics. In 2017 she was shortlisted for the Bridport Prize and a winner of the Persimmon International Poets Competition. Her poem 'Mercy' was highly commended by The Hedgehog Poetry Press and published in *The Road to Clevedon Pier* in 2018.

Nigel Kent

Nigel is a reader and writer of poetry who lives in Worcestershire. He has been shortlisted for a number of poetry prizes but has not yet won one! His poetry has been published by Hedgehog Poetry Press, Dempsey and Windle, Paper Swan Press, Emma's Attic Publishing, the Poetry Society of the Open University, Fly on the Wall Poetry Press and Eye Flash Poetry.
He generally writes free verse and is an admirer of the work of Ted Kooser, Steve Kowit, Stephen Dobyns, Gary Soto, Kim Addonizio, Maggie Sawkins, Luke Wright, Tony Walsh Michael Meyerhofer and , of course, Sarah Thomson! Currently he is working on a collection of poetry written in response to his favourite paintings.

www.ingramcontent.com/pod-product-compliance
Lightning Source LLC
Chambersburg PA
CBHW021135080526
44587CB00012B/1304